Foreword and Endorsei

A few years ago, I was asked the question, "What will be the greatest global challenge as we enter the 21st Century?" You may think of war, terrorism, famine, AIDS and a number of other colossal needs, which all surely qualify. But among the most serious issues is gender injustice – the abuse and suppression of women. Why? Because it is the biggest, most far reaching, and most hidden.

The Church needs to take a stand, the Church needs to raise its voice, the Church needs to pray and act, because God's heart breaks over gender injustice.

Just as the Apostle Paul commended Phoebe in Romans 16:1, I would like to commend to you Paul & Susi Childers, who are heading up an initiative to mobilize the Church to pray and act regarding gender injustice. God has called them to be a "voice for the voiceless," and they are using their voices to call others to join them.

Paul and Susi embody a unique combination of communication gifts specially designed by God to express His heart for those who can't communicate for themselves. Both are grounded in the Word and have anointed public speaking ministries. They exude a passion for God and His world. But one of the things that gives them an authority to speak about God's heart regarding global issues of injustice is that they KNOW the world. By the end of his 20s, Paul had traveled around the globe in ministry more times than most people travel around their nation. And Susi, a professional photographer who uses her camera to capture the intrinsic value of each individual, has trekked into some of the most remote and unreached peoples of Africa, the Middle East and the Amazon.

I heartily commend Paul and Susi to you as ones who have heard the heart of God for women, and who echo His call to help set them free to worship Him.

Loren Cunningham
Founder, Youth With A Mission
Kailua-Kona, Hawaii

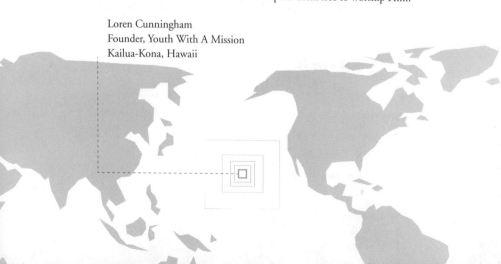

A note from the editors

If you have read this far, you are probably pretty determined to pursue this journey. Be warned. You will be challenged personally. We have not backed away from speaking directly about some of the most private and painful issues that impact voiceless women.

You may find yourself getting angry or upset. We believe that God himself experiences these emotions. He is grieved and angered over the impact of sin. However, the point of this booklet is not to raise negative emotion. It is to issue a call to prayer and action.

Our goal with this booklet is to mobilize 100,000 Christians around the world to pray and take action over a 30-day period. If successful we will have been involved in a prayer movement that will have lasted 24 hours a day, 7 days a week for 28.5 years.

You will notice that each day has five elements.

◼ First there is a **photograph.** Please take time to let the image speak to you.

◼ A brief **definition** with **facts** and **statistics** follow. Please see the endnotes at the back of the book for further study.

◼ Then comes the **personal impact story.** These stories, although based on fact, should not be considered biographical. In the early stages of this project, we made a strategic decision to write creatively and to protect people's privacy.

◼ Next come the **prayer points.** Please take 5 minutes to ponder the topic in prayer.

◼ Finally there are **action points.** As you begin to act, you will become part of the struggle against gender-based injustice. Although our actions may seem small, they will "echo in eternity."

There are several ways you can pray:

◼ Take one topic per day for 30 days in your private time with God.

◼ Select certain topics for your cell group. Discuss and pray through the issues.

◼ Take one issue each week and pray together in a church prayer group.

◼ Discuss several of these issues in your prayer breakfasts.

We hope you enjoy this prayer journey.

Paul and Susi Childers
Youth With A Mission
Kailua-Kona, Hawaii

Contents

Child Prostitution

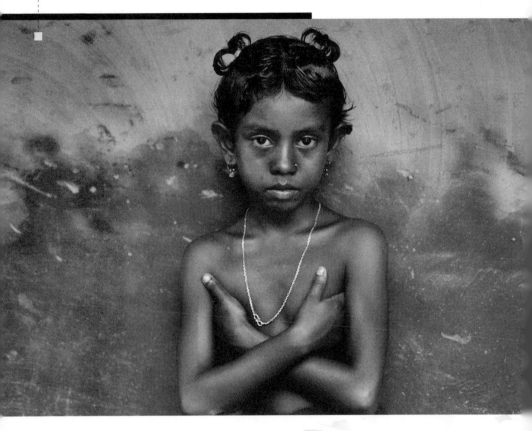

Definition
It is the sexual exploitation of a child for renumeration in cash or kind, usually but not always organized by an intermediary (parent, family member, procurer or teacher).[1]

- 10 million children worldwide are engaged in some facet of the sex industry. Each year at least one million children, mostly girls, become prostitutes.[2]

- In Thailand, 10-12 year old girls service men in the sex industry. They typically have sex with men 10-15 times daily and sometimes as many as 20-30.[3]

- In South Africa, there are 40,000 child prostitutes.[4]

- Children are more susceptible to HIV and other STDs.[5]

Personal Impact Story

Her family needed food and Prema's father had few other options. She was the eldest daughter, beautiful, and at eleven years old, more useful to the family away in the city of Mumbai. One less mouth to feed. One less body to clothe. Prema's mother, with tears in her eyes, promised they would see her again. Promised they would buy her back with the money Prema made every month – money her new guardian would send to the family. A promise made to Prema two and a half years ago.

In the city, Prema is not chained to a desk or forced to hunch over menial work for hours each day like thousands of other children throughout the developing world. Prema dances at a pole, bats her eyelashes at adults who have come from all over the world to watch her. She spreads her legs and moves her body to music, the way the other girls showed her. Girls kidnapped from their homes when they were younger or sold by their parents to the brothel.

As Prema waits to return to her family, other promises are kept. Her guardian makes good on the promise he made to her parents that she would be well looked after. Men, some older than her father, foreigners with unusual accents, take great delight in watching her dance on the stage. Then they pay to suffocate her under their heavy bodies. The guardian fulfills his promise that Prema would not be denied an education. He, along with his clients, tutor her in a whole new language with it's own, intricate vocabulary. Along with the other girls in the brothel, Prema has learned to say once-foreign words: *HIV, unwanted pregnancy, rape.*

Prema dances at her pole, learning a new language. Day after day she tries to remember the sound of her mother's voice, and waits to see if her parents will make good on their promise.

Because of the oppression of the weak and the groaning of the needy, GOD will now arise. Ps. 12:5

pray
- **that God would arise and defend the little ones**
- **that God would raise up lawyers, moviemakers and government rulers who will bring an end to this savage exploitation**

act
Make a short presentation on the prevalence of child prostitution and how your government could take action. Share this in your church, work place, and circle of influence.

PrayerDay : 1

AIDS

Definition
Acquired Immune Deficiency Syndrome (AIDS) is a serious, fatal disease of the immune system contracted through blood transfusions, sexual contact or contaminated needles. There is no known cure for it.[1]

- AIDS has killed more than 25 million people since 1981 – more than four Jewish holocausts or 22 Rwandan genocides.[2]
- In 2005, every minute there were 10 newly infected people worldwide.[3]
- Africa has 12 million AIDS orphans.[4]
- 43% of those infected with HIV are women.[5]
- There are 40.3 million people living with HIV/AIDS worldwide, a 1/3 are between the ages of 15 -24 .[6]

Personal Impact Story

In a small village in Mozambique, Zorah wakes up early to begin her work: caring for her three children, her aging father-in-law, and harvesting the fields. Since her husband's death a month ago, responsibility has fallen entirely on her. She is tired, but she says nothing, only gathers up a basket of dirty clothes before heading down to the riverbank to wash.

A doctor who visits the village every week told Zorah that her husband died of AIDS. She didn't know her husband was infected with a virus called HIV when she married him. She didn't know that he knew he was sick. At the time, she was 16 and he 31. She didn't know he believed that sleeping with a virgin would cure his disease.

She didn't know that using a condom might have protected her from infection, and if she had known, what difference would it have made? She and her husband never talked about sex; he simply demanded it from her. Sometimes he was rough with her, and she would bleed. She didn't know that increased her vulnerability of contracting the disease.

The sun is coming up over the horizon, glinting on the slow-moving ripples that mark the river's constant current. Zorah washes a shirt. Her chest hurts, and a dry cough has been troubling her for the past week. This morning she feels feverish and her body is aching. Her husband's illness started out the same way. Within a year he was dead. Zorah wrings out the last shirt as she gazes across the water. She didn't know about AIDS before, but she does now. She knows that it will kill her too. She knows there is currently no cure. She knows her family will be left alone. She doesn't know who will care for them.

The tears on her cheeks catch the light of the rising sun. She does not cry for long – her family is waiting, and they are hungry. She picks up the basket of wet clothes and begins the long, slow walk over the dirt road that leads back home.

God delights in showing mercy. Micha 7:18b

pray

■ **that God would intervene against this epidemic**

■ **that he would raise up medical researchers and doctors to discover solutions to HIV**

■ **that God would release Bible teachers to confront the causes of AIDS to see personal and social transformation**

act

Research the impact AIDS has on the nation of Botswana.

Prayer**Day** : 2

Domestic Violence

Definition

Domestic violence occurs between spouses or intimate partners, when one partner in the relationship tries to control the other person. The perpetrator uses fear and intimidation and often physical or sexual violence.[1]

■ One out of three women worldwide has been beaten, coerced into sex, or otherwise abused in her lifetime.[2]

■ 4 million women a year are assaulted by their partners. In 1 of 4 cases, women will also experience sexual abuse.[3]

■ 60% of battered women are abused while they are pregnant.[4]

■ 70-90% of women in Pakistan experience domestic violence.[5]

■ Every 9 seconds in the United States, a woman is assaulted and beaten.

■ 1.1 million women in Australia have experienced violence by a previous partner.[6]

Personal Impact Story

His words cut into her. Foul words, jagged and careless. Words that knock the wind right out of her. More so than any fist, his words leave her stunned. Stunned at his viciousness. Stunned at his cruelty. Stunned because tomorrow she won't see any signs that he is a monster, but will look exactly like the man that she married, the man she loves.

She's your neighbor. No matter what language you speak or where you live – a house in Peru, an apartment in Toronto, or a hut in a North African village. You talk to her throughout the week, send your kids outside to play with her kids, you share the same street.

She is a housewife and her husband hits her, beats the health and spirit right out of her. Oh, how he swings, until her body bleeds, until her muscles tear, until bones crack. She takes blow after blow because her husband drinks too much, had a bad day at work, because she will take a beating to keep him from the children, because she cannot, no matter how she tries, please him.

You may not have seen the bruise marks or swelling that cover her body, wounds she so expertly hides. You don't know that she cut her beautiful long hair so her husband has less leverage with which to swing her head and smash it against the floor, the toilet, the wall. You may not know how her stomach tightens or how her breathing stops whenever men are nearby. You may not know that she wishes to scream and rage and fight because she lives daily in fear for her own life. She is tormented by the risk of wishing she could run away with the children, go to the emergency room, or call the police.

She is your neighbor and at night she cries and hurts and bleeds.

Defend the cause of the weak. Ps. 83:2

- **for the protection of women who face domestic violence**
- **that God would stir His people to raise the standard of mutual respect in marriage**
- **that God would raise up men who can mentor others how to be godly husbands and fathers**

Discuss with your friends how wide spread domestic violence is in your town and think of ways how your church could contribute to a solution.

Prayer**Day** : 3

Pakistan

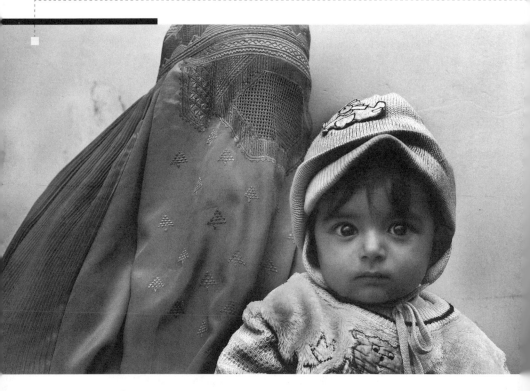

Definition

Pakistan has over 81 million women who suffer some of the worst cases of gender-based injustice. Female literacy is 23%; school enrollment is 16%; maternal mortality rate is as high as 340 per 100,000 live births.[1]

■ 99% of the babies which are thrown into gutters, trash bins and on sidewalks in Karachi are girls. They are considered a burden to society.[3]

■ Nearly 50% of women who do report rape are jailed due to an ordinance which doesn't recognize rape in a marriage.[4]

■ Pakistani men killed 280 women and disfigured 750 in 2002 from intentional acid attacks.[5]

■ Daily up to three women die from "stove deaths;" one out of three of these were pregnant. This usually occurs after a history of marital abuse for not giving birth to a son, disobedience, or allegations of adultery.[6]

Personal Impact Story

In a cramped, airless cell, Zafran Bibi, 28, sits listlessly in semi-darkness with her seven-month-old baby daughter. A fan slowly churns high above her head, barely stirring the stifling heat. Zafran Bibi is in the "condemned" ward. She has been sentenced to death by stoning for adultery.

In a sense, this won't be her first death. She has been forced to live in degrading conditions, deprived of her dignity. This cell has no lavatory. An overpowering stench hangs in the air. Each day her tiny window is opened for half an hour. Her food is worse even than that served to the regular inmates. Like the other condemned prisoners, she cannot wear an izarband, lest she hang herself with it. The ward is a man-made hell.

Zafran Bibi was married 13 years ago to Naimat Khan. Three years into their marriage he was convicted of murder and sentenced to 25 years. She had to live with her in-laws, harassed occasionally by her husband's brother, Jamal. When she complained about his advances her mother-in-law blamed her. A few days later Jamal raped Zafran. Her in-laws discovered she was pregnant and accused her of adultery with another man called Akmal Khan. This got Jamal off scot free, and Akmal was thrown into jail.

Zafran still went to the police with her father-in-law to file a report. She stated that she was raped while cutting grass a short distance from her house. But even her own lawyer portrayed her in court as a woman of low character involved willingly in a sexual relationship. She got death by stoning for her ungodly behavior while the rapist was released.

The reputation of a woman's chastity and purity must be preserved at all costs for the honor of the family.

God will judge the world in righteousness Ps. 9:8

pray

- that God would restore the dignity of women who are victims of a distorted code of honor
- that he would raise up righteous officials to enforce the laws of the land
- for the protection of Pakistani women

act

Research a story of a Pakistani woman affected by the honor system. Reflect on the price of honor.

PrayerDay : 4

Abortion

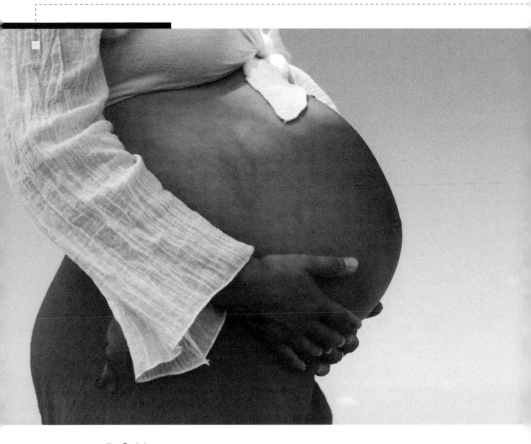

Definition
It is the medical termination of a pregnancy at any point before the full delivery of the baby.

- Approximately 46 million abortions take place each year worldwide – 126,000 abortions per day, 87 each minute, almost 2 every 3 seconds.[2]

- The average is 1 abortion per woman worldwide.[3]

- In many developing countries, abortion is accepted as a primary birth control method.[4]

- Careless abortions account for 80,000 maternal deaths globally per year.[5]

- Approximately 6.4 million abortions occur annually in the U.S.[6]

Personal Impact Story

Tears fill Jenny's eyes. She lies on the bed, bent over in pain. I ask her to describe her dream:

"Put your ear to the earth. Listen. Do you hear how they cry out?"
The woman who says this stands in front of me on the hill, she is dressed in white and a veil covers her face. I hesitate at first. Slowly, I place both hands on the ground. When I put my ear to the ground, the earth goes cold.

I hear a sound, faint and frightening, like voices screaming underwater. I close my eyes, trying to make out the words. When I hear what the voices say, I am, terrified. I open my eyes and look toward the woman, but she is gone.

A strong wind blows my hair into my face. Disoriented, I look at the ground and I scream when I realize that tiny little bodies cover the ground. Babies! Soon I realize that the bodies are the ground: fingers, limbs, discarded body parts as far as I can see. Mounds of little, dead bodies, an entire landscape of human remains.

I want to run, but can't move. I want to scream, but have no voice. Suddenly the wind stops. I look to the ground again, and in unison, thousands of little heads turn toward me. Some heads are not fully formed, lack eyes sockets, others have bleeding, open wounds. Then they speak. Their words stop my breath – the voices I heard deep inside the earth:
"Give us our souls. Return our stolen years."

I faint into dark dreams, and when I wake, the woman stands in front of me again. There is a gaping hole where her stomach used to be, empty and dark like a cave. Blood flows out from the wound and down her legs. She removes her veil and my heart stops. I'm looking into my own face. The woman, somehow, is me. She smiles weakly and says, "We have added to the dead."

I move to help her as she falls into my arms. She closes her eyes, whispers, "There are so many."

Jenny turns in the bed and looks at me.
"Don't worry, Jenny," I say, "it was only a dream."

God delights in forming babies in their mother's womb. Ps. 139:13

pray

p r a y
- ■ that God's broken heart for aborted babies would become the conscience of the world
- ■ that laws valuing life over choice would be written and enforced in your nation

a c t **Write to your local politician expressing your outrage about abortion and give ideas how the law can be changed.**

Prayer**Day** : 5

Refugees

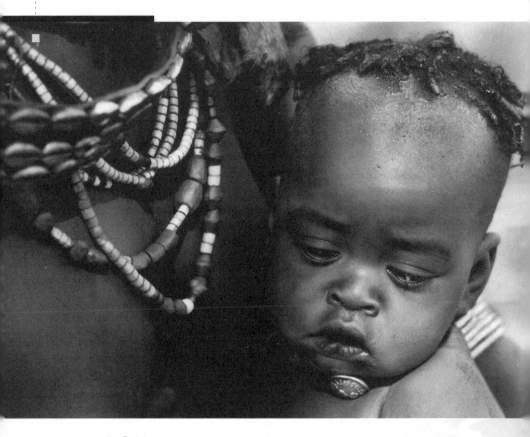

Definition
A refugee is a person who flees his/her home to escape invasion, oppression, or persecution. They genuinely risk serious human rights abuses.[1]

- There are about 10.6 million refugees and 25.8 million internally displaced people (IDP) worldwide.[2]

- 75-80% of the world's refuges are women and children.[3]

- Women and children refugees are vulnerable to violence and exploitation by military and immigration personnel, bandit groups, male refugees and rival ethnic groups.[4]

- Asia and Africa host the majority of the world's refugees and 18.1 million IDPs.[5]

Personal Impact Story

Six days in the camp and already Hawa has five questions answered. Soon the form will be full and Hawa and her children will be granted *asylum*: a word she, at first, did not understand. Hawa thought when she arrived at the refugee camp that her children would have food, and that the fear would stop. But the camp is filled with panic and the memory of cruel men. Men who killed and displaced entire families to gain pride, power and racial purity.

One of the girls she met in the long line for food asked Hawa where she was from. The girl was the first kind face in an unfamiliar and strange country. She had fled from the fighting in Sudan as well, with her uncle and brother. The girl told Hawa that if she and her children wanted safety inside Chad, she would need *asylum*. That's why Hawa agreed to visit the girl's uncle who helped people like Hawa: women who couldn't read or write. *Asylum* is why Hawa agreed to his price, only because she needed his help to complete the form.

If Hawa had learned to read and write, she would have printed, in neat, clean letters of her own:

Name: Hawa Fentale
Sex: Female
Age: 24
Country of Origin: Sudan
Family Members: Husband (deceased)
                      2 Children (female: aged 3; male: 8 months old)

But Hawa cannot write. She can only look at the government form that weighs heavily in her hand and wonder what other questions remain. Hawa waits through the night unaware that there is a child growing in her womb, a child that does not belong to her dead husband. Between pangs of hunger and cries from her children, Hawa imagines what life will hold when her family is given asylum in Chad, and how as a stranger and a widow she will find a home. In the morning, she will bring the white government form to the girl's uncle again and pay his price so she can answer another question.

GOD is compassionate. Ex. 34:6

pray

- **that God would comfort displaced people, heal their memories and give them a new home to live**
- **that the churches would reach out and open their homes and hearts to immigrants and refugees** Lev 19:34

act

Approach an immigrant this week in your city and listen to her story.

Prayer**Day** : 6

Eating Disorders

Definition

An eating disorder is a compulsion where a person's eating habits damage their health. The eating may be too excessive (compulsive overeating), too limited (restricting), or cycles of binging and purging.[1]

- Up to 70 million people worldwide struggle with eating disorders, 90-95% of whom are women.[2]

- 95% of those who have eating disorders are between the ages of 12 and 25.[3]

- Eating disorders have been diagnosed in girls as young as seven. 81% of 10-year olds in the United States are afraid of being fat.[4]

- The average American woman is 5'4" tall and weighs 140 pounds. The average American model is 5'11" tall and weighs 117 pounds.[5]

Personal Impact Story

It is her secret life and soon they will know it, when her mom finds her body, lifeless on the floor. Every day she stands in front of the mirror doing an inventory of her imperfect body, unable to look herself in the eye, disgusted with herself.

She thinks the problem is her body, but really it is her mind. She cannot see how thin she has become with self-hatred, how the skin of her face pulls tightly over cheekbones and eye sockets, how her hips have all but disappeared. She is miserable at the sight of herself, always unsatisfied, seeing herself as "too fat" when in reality, she has brought herself almost to a point of weightlessness. She cannot hear her body's groaning; she has made it hungry but will no longer feed it.

She remembers the first time she put her fingers in the back of her throat, heart beating anxiously and how the fingers were like a gun and she hesitantly pushed the weapon further down her throat. Then suddenly her stomach was empty. She had been afraid at first, but it was simple and painless, really. The next day it was easier, she knew what to expect, knew that her stomach would cramp and tighten as she bent over the toilet, that if she ran water at the sink people in the house could not hear. It was her little secret. She told herself she would only do it a few times a week, would continue exercising and only purge occasionally, just as a way to help her body rid itself of calories, to get control of the fat before the fat took control of her.

She stands in front of the mirror, staring at herself, fingers ready at her side. She is only one girl among millions who have skimmed through fashion magazines, overheard fat jokes, who have been treated poorly by boyfriends, failed at dieting, who have suffered sexual abuse from uncles, fathers, or complete strangers. One of many millions of hungry, beautiful girls who stare at their bodies, unable to see their beauty.

And tomorrow she will die.

pray
GOD delights in his daughters. Zeph. 3:17

p r a y
- **that the affected girls would discover the delight God has in them**
- **that they would comprehend what true beauty is**
- **for the church to address this growing issue**

a c t
Discuss this topic with a teenage girl and get to know her ideas about beauty and fashion.

PrayerDay : 7

Purdah

Definition
Purdah is the practice of the seclusion of women from public observation by covering their bodies from head to toe. It is also a state of social isolation, which confines women to their homes.[1]

- Purdah is seen as a protection of the dignity of women.[2]

- In some cases, segregation is taken so seriously that houses are surrounded with eight to ten foot high purdah walls.[3]

- Purdah is frequently carried to such extremes that women suffer from softening of bones, eczema and ulcers due to a lack of sunlight.[4]

- In Bangladesh, women have been attacked with acid because they were brave enough to be seen in public, transgressing the traditional boundaries of purdah.[5]

- Purdah includes the restriction of women's access to medical care.[6]

see   know   feel   pray   do

Personal Impact Story

Nailah's destiny was predetermined by her culture before she pushed her way through the dark birth passage, before the umbilical cord was cut and her lungs wakened with her first breath of air. Her fate was the same as all of the other women in her village. By the time of puberty Nailah would have to be covered from head to toe. Sunlight would be a rare priviledge and even medical care would be limited. Her mother would teach her what it means to submit and, in her early years she will learn how to obey a man's voice.

As Nailah entered the world, mourning and disappointment were all around her. Rejection was written all over their faces. Her father's pursed lips, silent curse; Grandmother and the other women's shoulders rigid, frozen in silence, heads bowed, looking at the ground; Uncle kissing father's cheek, holding him by the shoulders, whispering; Grandfather, with tears in his eyes. Nailah's birth was a disaster because she was a girl.

Mother's faceless face, covered in dark cloth; another passage and another birth awaiting Nailah. A covering to surround Nailah like the placenta that followed her out of her mother's body like a shadow, that once held her, hid her from her family's expectant view. A layer to shadow her whole life behind the walls meant to protect her modesty and the family's honor, behind closed doors and separate chambers. A new skin to cover her skin, to hide it from the sun, from the wind, from roving eyes, the unchaste. A dark layer to hide her tears and the smile few will ever see.

More sacrifices, more prayer, deeper submission, the resolve is written across father's face as he hands Nailah to grandmother who will take her into the room where the women stay. *Surely Allah in his goodness will give more sons.*

pray

Nothing is hidden from GOD's sight. Heb. 4:13a

■ that God would break down the walls of segregation so women would be released into their destinies

■ for doctors to speak up about the physical consequences of purdah on a government level

■ for the release of female missionaries to serve these women

act

For 48 hours log every time you leave home and record what you did. Reflect how different your life would be if you were confined to your home.

PrayerDay : 8

Female Laborers

Definition

Female laborers are women who work too long, too hard and too much, especially in back breaking manual labor.

- Out of the 550 million working poor in the world, an estimated 330 million, or 60%, are women.[1]

- The majority of women earn on average about 3/4 of the pay of males for the same work.[2]

- An African peasant woman typically works 16 hours daily trudging long distances to fetch firewood, animal fodder and water, growing and harvesting food, tending crops, and cooking and caring for her family. This leaves little time to seek education and training, the very things that enable women to break the cycle of low status and poverty.[3]

- Worldwide, over 60% of people working in family enterprises without pay are women.[4]

- On a one hectare farm in the Indian Himalayans, a pair of bullock's works 1064 hours, a man works 1212 hours and a woman 3485 hours in a year.[5]

Personal Impact Story

The women of the village would laugh about it, look up from their work as they cooked around the fire, and push their tongues through spaces once filled by teeth and smile. They tried to prepare me for the day when the village midwife would put a knife between my legs and cut me.

"You'll scream until you fade into dark dreams, then wake up groaning in pain. The most pain you will ever know."

"You'll pray to God that you could die. It is one of the times in your life you'll wish you were born a man."

"But, you won't have to do any work for a week." And then they would all laugh. Around the circle they would go, energized by each other's playfulness after another tiring day, each new comment like another stick thrown on the fire, until they felt warmed and comforted by laughter.

"A week of rest, of sleeping, of nothing."

"You'll feel restless with so little to do."

"But oh, you'll remember that week, daughter. When you're out in the field planting seeds with your own hands, bent over the dry earth."

"When you're walking all that way from the river with a jug of water on your head, the sun beating down on you."

"When you're fetching firewood, or watering the goats."

"When your husband chooses to lie with you at night – "

"Or in the morning, or in the afternoon!"

"When you bury another baby in the ground, you'll remember that week of rest." The women sitting around the fire would become quiet. Some busy again with work. Some would stare into the fire. Their faces betrayed their fatigue. Skin weathered by wind and dryness and sun. Bodies taut, hands strong and muscled.

"You'll wish there was more skin left to cut, daughter. There will be days when you will wish you were thirteen again and that you could feel that cold flint knife against your thigh. You'll wish you could bite that stick between your teeth and welcome the pain, if only to have a few days of rest."

Who is like our God who rescues the poor from those too strong for them? Ps. 35:10

pray
- this verse over the exploited women who are forced to work too long, too hard, too much
- for godly business owners
- for Bible based family structures

act **Reflect on the biblical concept of work and appropriate rest. Apply it in your life.**

Prayer**Day** : 9

China

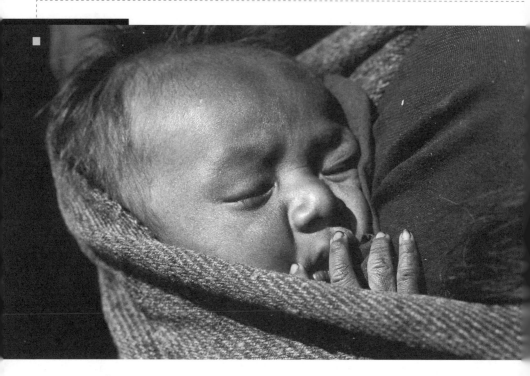

Definition

China is the world's most populated country with over 1.3 billion people, 637.5 million of which are women.[1]

- For centuries, Chinese families without sons feared poverty and neglect. The male offspring represents continuity of lineage and protection in old age.[2]

- The age-old bias towards boys, combined with the one-child policy imposed since 1980, has produced the largest, the highest, and the longest gender imbalance in the world.[3] The male surplus rose to 120 boys for each 100 girls.[4]

- Predictions for the next decade are that some 40 million Chinese men will be unable to find wives due to the "scarcity" of females as a result of kidnapping, trafficking and selective abortions.[5]

- Women, who are up to 9 months pregnant with their second or third baby, may be taken to the hospital by regional population control officials for induced abortions.[6]

Personal Impact Story

Daughter,

Great distance has separated us for twenty-two years. I write slowly. I try to remember your face. A true Chinese face, round, and dignified.

I have buried the memory of you deeply within. My heart feels like a hardened tomb, cold, filled with no light. But every year around this time, the time of your birth, a memory tremors through my body, sharper, more painful than the contractions that delivered you into our cruel world.

Auntie An-wa told me it would help if I did not think to name you, if I imagined your birth a still-birth the moment we discovered you were not a boy. Her first child was also a girl; she had it soon after the government made their decision to allow only one child for each family. But I named you anyway, the name of a flower I learned about at school.

Your father was so excited that day, he was sure you would be a boy. We drove hours by bus a week before your arrival, winding through rice fields so we could get help from a better doctor. Your father held me to the bed, buried his face in my chest, cried with me after he quietly nodded his head at the doctor who took you out of the room.

Your face: oval eyes, high cheekbones, and flat nose. I see it a thousand times, on every street, in every shop, every temple. But it is not your face. You are not here with me. My beloved Violet, flower of my womb, joy of my heart for one day, pulled from me and taken away.

I wanted to scream at the doctor, "Just one!" That's all you were, just one more girl, surely there would have been room and food enough in this country. But no. It is a cruel world. Who am I to defy its rules?

Today would be your birthday, daughter. You would be twenty-two years old. I will hide this letter with all the others I have written, forget you for a time. It's too painful to live remembering you.

GOD created man in his own image... male and female he created them. Gen. 1:27

pray
- God created man and women equal. Pray that God would reveal this truth to the Chinese culture
- that China will stop its one-child policy
- that lives would be valued in new measure

act
Discuss with two friends the implications of male bias coupled with the one-child policy. Find out how to support Christian adoption agencies in China.

Incest

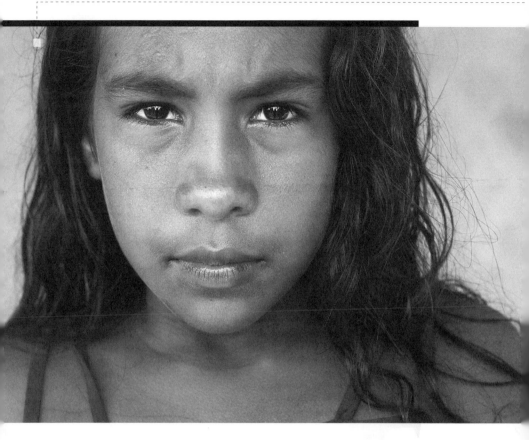

Definition

Sexual intercourse or other sexual activity between persons so closely related that marriage between them is legally or culturally prohibited.[1]

■ 90 - 95% of all sexual abuse cases go unreported to the police.[2] 94% of child rape victims under the age of 12 were abused by a family member or an acquaintance.[3]

■ 68% of incest survivors were adult victims of rape or attempted rape.[4]

■ In East Africa 9 out of 10 girls are abused by the people who they trust most.

■ 36.7% of all women in prison in the U.S. were abused as children.[6] 66% of all prostitues are victims of child sexual abuse.[7]

■ One third of abused and neglected children will later abuse their own children.[8]

Personal Impact Story

"You're a woman now, Anna." By this, her uncle means that she can be kicked, mutilated, sold like a commodity, burnt at the stake, raped. "You're a woman now, Anna," says her uncle.

Anna wakes from her dream, heart racing. She wants to sleep for a year, but she can't for fear of the memory. Anna kneels beside her bed to pray. She's been in the city for six months. She ran away from the farm that night. She told herself any place, any home, would be better, safer. The words come clumsily, she hasn't prayed in awhile, almost forgets how.

When Anna closes her eyes to pray, the memory plays out in her mind, the nightmare of that night forces itself upon her against her will. All at once she is on her uncle's farm again, in the barn. There to see the new litter of kittens her uncle said were born early that morning. Before she can ask him where the kittens are, his hand is on her shoulder.

She can smell the oil and gasoline on her uncle's shirt as he moves to wipe his forehead. A line of black from his dirty hand trails under his hairline.

There are no kittens. Then it all happens. Quickly. He grabs her by each arm and pushes her into the hay. The scream is sucked out of her chest as she is pushed harder against the ground. Her voice is trapped somewhere between her stomach and her heart. She can't pull away.

That is where her memory lets it stop, lying there, cold and trembling on the ground, voiceless. Even her mother refused to believe her. She ran out of the house, vowing never to return. The night that changed her life, the night she ran away to the city.

Anna is on her knees again. This time she is praying. "God, make me a virgin again," she mumbles. The men who pay like to think she is one.

pray

GOD is called 'El-Roi', the GOD who sees all. Gen. 16:13
- **that God would bring justice to the victims of incest**
- **for the protection and health of children who live under this threat**
- **that this hidden sin would be exposed and eliminated**

act

Find a children's shelter in your city and volunteer for a day. Listen to a story of a victim.

PrayerDay : 11

Barren Women

Definition
A woman incapable of conceiving or unable to get pregnant.[1]

- 50-80 million people worldwide suffer from infertility.[2]

- The impact of infertility is compounded because women are generally held responsible for reproductive failure. This blame may result in divorce, husbands taking a second wife, difficulties with in-laws, domestic violence and economic abandonment.[3]

- In some places motherhood is the only way for women to enhance their status within the family and community.[4]

- A sad reality of infertility is that it's causes are largely preventable such as sexually transmitted diseases, poor hygiene and harmful health care practices.[5]

- Infections occur in 70% of abortions. If not stopped soon enough, they can leave a woman barren.[6]

Personal Impact Story

I am barren. Every month I hold my breath and say a prayer – many prayers – and every month the turning moon mocks my fragile hopes as it calls forth another river of blood. Oh God, what would I give to stem that implacable tide!

I am despised by men who don't see any purpose for me apart from bearing children. I am pitied by women who are more favored than I, and of whom I am jealous with an intensity that sometimes borders on madness. I am utterly alone, and full of emptiness that devours me from the inside out – a long, slow, agonizing death of the heart. Little by little I am being eaten alive, and one day there will be nothing left.

Empty womb, empty arms, empty heart. I am a dry stick, a withered vine, a hollow tree. My body is a vast promise unfulfilled.

I watch helpless as my husband's eye follow the movements of younger women. I have dishonored him by not producing a son. He will divorce me soon. I try not to think about where I will go, what I will do. I have no schooling, no education. My parents will not take me back – I am no longer their responsibility.

Every morning I wake up and pray that I will have a roof over my head for one more day. Sometimes I pray that my husband will love me, but I would be happy if he would simply not beat me or scream at me for not giving him the children that I am desperate to have. One son would dissolve my shame forever. It seems such a little thing to ask of heaven.

But my prayer falls to the ground. Too many have gone unanswered.

GOD blessed man and woman and commanded them to be fruitful and multiply. Gen. 1:28

pray
- that God would raise up Christian leaders in traditional cultures to speak about the true value of women
- for "miracle" babies

act Invite a childless couple to your home for dinner. Listen to their story. Affirm their value. **Pray** Psalm 115:14 **over them.**

PrayerDay : 12

Pornography

Definition
Pornography is the explicit depiction of sexual activity in literature, films, photography, or the internet, that stimulates erotic feelings.[1]

■ The pornography industry is a $57 billion global business, $12 billion of this is in the US. This is larger than the combined revenues of all professional football, baseball and basketball franchises in the US.[2]

■ Child pornography alone generates $3 billion annually and the average age for first internet exposure to pornography is 11.[3]

■ Globally 72 million people visit pornographic web sites each year – 200,000 every day.[4]

■ 47% of Christian men say pornography is a major problem in the home.[5]

■ A search in Google on the word 'porn' returned over 165 million pages, and 'xxx' returned more than 200 million.[6]

see   know   feel   pray   do

Personal Impact Story

He owns her. One move of his finger and she is his: beautiful, healthy, and young. He owns her, though he has never seen her before. A woman without a name. He likes it that way. Another woman he will add to the harem of his lust. One of many women who wait for him, quietly and patiently, in the dark storehouses of his mind. There they sit on display like bottles of liquor in a cabinet, ready to be poured out into the chalice of his desire and consumed.

She is a stranger to him, and already he feasts on her nakedness, knows every part of her body, the way she is stretched out before him. She pleases him because she is silent, willing, and asks for nothing in return. She does not show him the heart that beats behind her exposed breasts. She does not ask for his name, she does not care to know his age. She cannot demand flowers, ask for diamonds, or say the word "love." She lies before him, exposed and vulnerable. And she will stay there, in the same position, playing his game, pretending to desire him. She will not move until he tires of her and wants the promise of new flesh. He spent his pocket change, and now she belongs to him.

She will be invited onto the movie screen of his mind, loyal to him, as he trains his body and mind to think of her as an object to grope and ravage and touch. And then with a single movement of his finger, the flip of a page, she will be ushered back into the dark room of his memory. With the click of his finger at his computer, she will be filed and stored away. She will wait there until he tires of the other lovers, old and new: a fix, a stimulant. His beautiful lover without a name.

GOD is holy. Lev. 20:26

pray
- that God would send a spirit of conviction to the church about the evil of pornography
- that the internet would be regulated to marginalize pornography
- that law enforcement would break peadophile rings

act
Repent of any use of pornography in your life.
Write a letter to you local politicians expressing your concern with this matter.

PrayerDay : 13

Female Suicide Bombers

Definition
Women who are recruited to die with explosive belts strapped around their waists to kill others under the guise of equality, the promise of rehabilitating a family member, or cleansing their own reputations.[1]

■ Suicide bombers are today's weapons of choice because they are low on cost, technology, and risk and are readily available. They require little training, leave no trace behind, and strike fear into the general population.[2]

■ Female suicide bombers believe their destiny is to become the bride of Allah in paradise.[3]

■ "We have to defend ourselves with the only thing we have, our bodies. Our bodies are the only fighting means at our disposal." Hiba, 28, mother of five, suicide bomber trainee.[4]

■ Streets, hospitals, babies and children's events are named after "martyrs."[5]

Personal Impact Story

On a late autumn afternoon, a group of women walked the winding, narrow streets of al-Amari refugee camp. Guiding them was a young Palestinian man, from the local university. His eyes were dark and full of pain, even when he smiled.

They arrived at their destination and stepped into the tiny house. It took a moment for their eyes to adjust to the dim light. The living room was small, and had but one focus: a larger-than-life poster on the far wall, of a young woman's face adorned with a black-and-white headband. The gleaming Dome of the Rock dominated the background. This young woman was Wafa, enshrined in this humble home as a successful martyr.

On another wall were photos depicting scenes from Wafa's brief life: her graduation; her wedding; a group of Red Crescent workers (of which she was one). In the corner of the room sat a lady, covered with a dark scarf. Her name was Malbrook, and she was Wafa's mother. Malbrook was a little woman. Little and old. She did not look surprised to see her visitors, nor did she seem happy. "Ask her anything," said the guide to the women. "I will translate."

The women were awkwardly silent. Malbrook spoke a little about her daughter, spoke with pride, but there was something else in her voice and manner. She seemed weighted with sadness; a deep, abiding grief that she had never stopped carrying since the day she lost her daughter. Her voice was soft. She told the women that she still cried all the time, "day and night" for Wafa – who had died several years before.

One of the women went to Malbrook, and held her hand. She looked into the older woman's eyes as she knelt beside her. Then she prayed, never turning away her gaze. Tears flowed on more than one face in the room. "Did you know what she was going to do?" one of the women asked, referring to Wafa's plans to kill herself as a female suicide bomber.

"No," said her mother. "If I had known, I would have stopped her."

God is love. His gift is life. 1. John 4:8

p r a y
- that God would send visions and dreams of his love to women in danger of being recruited for suicide missions
- that God would meet these women in their desperation
- for more women missionaries to show them a better way

a c t **Find a chat room on the internet where you can contact Arab women. Explain the love of God to them shown in Jesus.**

PrayerDay : 14

Starvation

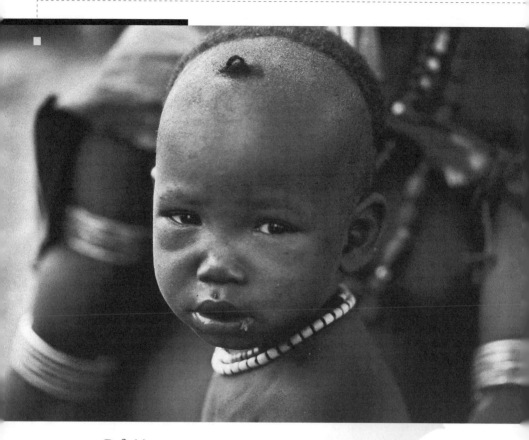

Definition

Starvation is a state of extreme hunger resulting from lack of essential nutrients over a prolonged period.[1]

- Globally over 9 million people die each year from hunger and malnutrition.[2]

- 6 million children under the age of 5 die every year from a hunger related cause. Every day, more than 16,000 children die – one child every five seconds.[3]

- About 850 million people globally are malnourished; 799 million of them live in the developing world. More than 153 million of them are children under the age of 5.[4]

- Gender is the most significant reason for malnutrition among young girls.[5]

- 54 nations currently do not produce enough food to feed their populations, nor can they afford to import the necessary commodities. Most of these countries are in sub-Saharan Africa.[6]

Personal Impact Story

She was born hungry. The first thought she ever had was food. The skin of her face wrinkled in frustration at her mother's dried up breast. She was unable to understand that her mother had no food to eat either, she was too young to be told her country has no food. Another hungry newborn: malnutrition and food shortage her birthright.

She would soon learn that tears could change nothing, no matter how many she poured out onto the ground. They would not sufficiently water the drought-ridden land to bring forth fruit. Fruit to feed her hungry family. The energy she spent to cry would only leave her with greater pangs of hunger.

Her mother at first did not name her, believing she would die like so many other newborns. But she lived. So she was named Mara – "bitterness" - for her life would be marked by a series of bitter rituals, rights of passage meant to measure her ability at survival. Her mother named her Mara knowing her little body would need to fight against other invisible predators hungry for her starving flesh: malaria, anemia, tuberculosis.

Mara's stomach is swollen and bloated by the final irony of starvation. Her empty stomach looks well fed, pushes itself out to the world as if were full of food. At three years old, she is pregnant with the hope of eating. She laughs when she is told that there are children in the world who are not born hungry. Surely, she thinks, there are men and boys who do not starve, who are fed food like the men and boys in her country.

But her mother insists that somewhere little girls do not starve, they eat three meals a day, smile and laugh regularly, and have energy left over to play. Girls who live in a land where there is food. Mara wonders what it would be like to see these strange girls, touch their chubby bellies, prod and poke in wonder that she cannot count each one of their ribs. She dreams of those little girls at night, and the thought of their bodies frightens her.

The LORD will grant you abundant prosperity in the crops of your ground. Deut. 28:11

pray
- thank God for the abundance you experience
- for farmers in developing countries that they learn how to cultivate their fields without stripping them of their fertility
- for fair distribution of food

act
Volunteer at a local food bank. Then discuss with several friends the main reasons for starvation and what your local community could do about it.

PrayerDay : 15

Trafficking

Definition

Trafficking is the "practice" of involuntarily moving people into locations and jobs for the profit of another. It consists of: violence, deception, coercion, deprivation of freedom of movement, abuse of authority, debt bondage, forced labor and slavery-like practices, and other forms of exploitation or use of force.[1]

- Human trafficking, sometimes called the "largest slave trade in history," is overtaking drug smuggling as one of the world's fastest growing illegal enterprises.[2]

- Worldwide trafficking numbers: 250,000 come from Asia, 100,000 from the former Soviet Union, 175,000 from Central and Eastern Europe, 100,000 from Latin America and the Caribbean, and 50,000 from Africa.[3] The majority of these victims are trafficked for commercial sexual exploitation. 80% are women and girls, and up to 50% are minors.[4] Iranian girls between 13 and 17 are victims of trafficking, some as young as 8 to10.[5]

- 120,000 women and children are trafficked into Western Europe every year. Many of these women are bought and sold into forced prostitution, beaten, imprisoned, raped, and sometimes killed.[6]

Personal Impact Story

"Stop dreaming, girl!" Victoria's mother barked. "You have to do the laundry, wash the dishes, change you brother's diapers…" Victoria's mind drifted off, "I've gotta get out of this place!" "Ok, mom", she responded. Her thoughts drift off again… teenagers in America have nice lives. She had seen it on cable TV. Maybe one day she could be a receptionist, a graphic designer or even a flight attendant. She had always loved the thought of travel. "I've gotta get out of Moldova," she resolved.

"You look like you're dreaming." Victoria looked up from her park bench, "My name is Tanja." "Hi", Victoria extended her hand to a well-dressed woman, "Yeah, I'm always dreaming of getting out of this hole. I want to go to America. I want to travel. I hate this place!" "Well today is your lucky day. I work for an American company in Turkey; we have an opening for a young woman. If you work hard enough, maybe you could get transferred to America! Corporate is always looking for new talent."

What a dream! As the fields sped by Victoria dreamed of her new flat in Istanbul, even a new boyfriend. "Get out of the car!" Her dream was rudely interrupted. "Why?" "Get out now and follow me". "But where are we?" "Now"! Victoria followed Tanja into a forested area. Men were waiting. A passport was thrust into her hands. The photo was familiar but the name was not hers. "You are coming with us now." After walking across the border into Serbia, Victoria was thrown to the ground. If you resist we will kill you, and nobody will know! Victoria was raped once, twice, by the third day she had lost count, lost her dignity and her will.

The dream was now a nightmare. Her captors sold her from brothel to brothel to satisfy the lust of desperate men. In two years she had been sold ten times, each time around $1,500 USD. Eventually she was sold into Albania. A client beats her in a urine smelling hotel. The neighbors complain. The police arrest Victoria for disturbing the peace. In her cell they rape her until they are finished. Then sell her on.

The nightmare now becomes a destiny. A child grows in her womb. Victoria clings to the dream that maybe her daughter will have a destiny in America…

pray

GOD looses the chains of injustice and unties the cords of the yoke, to set the oppressed free and break every yoke. Is.58:6
- ■ **this verse over all who are chained by trafficking**
- ■ **that news media would accurately and consistently portray this reality**

act

Research the prevalence of trafficking in your nation. Report the results to the government and to the media.

PrayerDay : 16

Afghanistan

Definition

Afghanistan has had over 20 years of war. It had an extreme fundamentalist government until 2001. Afghanistan is still unstable. It is one of the ten poorest countries in the world.[1] The female population is over 15 million.[2]

- ◼ 1-2% of Afghan women have identity cards; the rest are without formal papers or citizenship.[3]

- ◼ Life expectancy for women is 42 years of age.[4]

- ◼ Afghanistan is the only country worldwide to bar girls from secondary education. Schools for gi have been attacked and set on fire. Outside of Kabul, 91% of girls under 18 don't go to school

- ◼ 57% of girls marry before the age of 16.[6]

- ◼ "My father forcibly married me to an old man when I was 11 and my husband treated me like a slave over the last seven years." Zaynab, 18 Afghan mother of five.[7]

Personal Impact Story

She sat in the corner, watching the snow swirl. The cold from the window soothed her. The physical pain in her body matched the ache in her heart. Her mind turned again to her sisters and her mother. Only last winter she'd been with them. Her mother. How little she had understood her. The thought drifted through her like a snowflake. Meena felt the lump in her throat but her tears came seldom anymore.

She wondered again what life was really like in other countries. Girls could go to school they said. And they didn't marry so young. She would have her first child in a few more months. She'd been 11 when they told her she was to marry him, he thirty years her senior. She'd had no choice.

Her older sister had married at 14, only a few months before her. She'd moved to the next valley. Meena had heard about a cousin in the city who didn't marry until she was 18. Into a wealthy family they said. An honorable family with a traditional Afghan wedding that lasted four days. Of course Meena's family lived only in a small village. But the stories were still whispered to each other when the girls were alone.

Her thoughts were interrupted by the footsteps she heard approaching. A fist of fear struck her painfully. Would he beat her again because she wasn't working? She'd nearly fainted and had to sit down. Panic nearly choked her. "Ahmed!" a rough voice called. It wasn't him! Meena huddled closer to the wall and held her breath. "Ahmed!" Silence. The man muttered and turned away. She waited until his steps faded before she painfully scrambled to her feet and closed the window. She needed to do something quickly. He would be back any minute.

When GOD created man and woman he said that it was very good. Gen.1:31

pray
- **that Afghanis would grasp this truth**
- **that God would restore in Afghanistan his image, which is distorted through oppression and exploitation**
- **that God would send many workers into the harvest fields of this nation, especially educators and evangelists**

act
Find an NGO in Afghanistan that educates and assists women and children. See how you can help and support them.

PrayerDay : 17

Female Genital Mutilation

Definition

Female genital mutilation (FGM), often referred to as "female circumcision", comprises all procedures involving partial or total removal of the external female genitalia for cultural or religious reasons. This procedure is performed on females ranging from infancy to adolescence.[1]

■ 150 million women are victims of FGM. Every year 2 million girls are added. In Ethiopia 87% are circumcised, Djibouti 99%, Eritrea 98%, Somalia 98%, Sudan 95%.[2]

■ FGM can result in: extreme pain, shock from blood loss, gangrene in vulva tissues, tetanus from unsterilized equipment. Death can result from hemorrhage, blood poisoning, and acute urinary retention.[3]

■ The nations where FGM is practiced have the highest mother mortality rate in the world.[4]

■ For the average girl, there is no use of anesthetic or sterilized instruments in this procedure.[5]

Personal Impact Story

"Be brave, girl! You are a Somali woman!" her aunty commands. Strong hands pin her to the floor. Rough hands spread her legs. Screams pierce the air as a shard of glass expertly slices away immature womanhood. Thorns are all that this poor family has to stitch up the gaping wound. A hole the size of matchstick is left for urination and her menstruation in coming years. The operation is complete as they rub in a paste consisting of herbs, milk, eggs, ashes and dung. The perfect chastity belt is created.

"Be brave girl! Don't cry and he will like you," her mother advised. It is the night of her wedding. She had caught the eyes of the local butcher. It had been arranged quickly. He was 39 she was 14, but he paid well. As the music blared outside, he came to her. He was rough and thrusting. She was scared. It hurt. Her vaginal opening was too small. Lie still! She faints as he slices her open. In the morning she regains consciousness. He is gone. She looks down. There are bloody sheets. Her blood. She is re-stitched with a larger hole to allow easy access. The butcher continues to come to her until life begins in her womb.

"Be brave, girl! You may have a son," the midwife encourages. She is 15 now and proud to be able to give birth. Contractions seize her slight frame. She screams. The child is obstructed. Her vaginal scar prevents the butcher's child from coming. She must be opened. Again her vaginal scar is sliced open. She is able to keep conscious this time. She pushes and finally out comes a girl. "Oh well, no need for celebrations," the butcher thinks. It is just another mouth to feed. As an afterthought the mid-wife picks up needle and thread. The girl must be re-stitched. She needs to be tight for her husband once again.

So the brave girl develops into a brave woman. By her seventh child there is no more skin to stitch. But she bore the butcher three sons. Tomorrow her daughter comes of age. She will get up early and gather the women. Her first-born will be another brave Somali woman.

Our bodies are to be treated as temples. 1. Cor. 6:19

pray

- **that God would give revelation that every part of a woman's body is clean and created for a purpose**
- **that the church, educators and the media would work towards the elimination of this custom**
- **for the release of missionaries to minister to these women**

act **Discuss with three friends the implications of FGM. Let your ambassador to the United Nations know of your concern.**

Prayer**Day** : 18

Teenage Mothers

Definition
A teenage mother is a female aged 13-19 that has given birth to a child.

◼ In America about 1 million girls between the ages of 15 and 19 become pregnant each year; 1 in every 10 births worldwide is to a mother who is herself still a child.[1]

◼ Globally, 1 million children born to teenage mothers die before their first birthday each year while 70,000 teenage mothers die due to complications in childbirth.[2]

◼ In Niger more than 50% of girls aged 15-19 are married. 1 in 4 has given birth, and 1 out of 6 of their babies dies before reaching age 1.[3]

◼ Educated girls tend to marry later, have fewer children, and raise healthier, better-nourished children. They also are more likely to send their children to school.[4]

Personal Impact Story

If the child inside her young womb could speak, it might ask her a few questions. He grows inside her body, can hear the rhythm of her heart and senses that troubled heart's questions too. He might ask this first-time mother how she will care for him if she chooses to carry him full term, what she will do if she brings him into the world. Her body will continue to change, has swelled already with the new life inside of her, but life will not wait for her to adjust. Her high school friends will continue studying, socializing, busying themselves with all the important and meaningless things teenagers do. But she will have a new, helpless boy to love and feed to change and protect.

The child growing inside of her might ask – if she decides she does not want to be a teenager and a mom – whether or not she will name him before he is ripped out of her womb. He might think about the boy or man he could have become, had his lungs filled with breath in her mysterious, spinning world. He might wonder how that one, clean incision will feel as it cuts through the soft tissue of his skull. He could ask her if she will feel that one last kick, when his foot hits the protective wall of her uterus as his heart stops beating.

The unborn, unnamed child might say, "Mother, how will you care for yourself, will you drop out of school? Will you pay the bills? If I am born, will my life only remind you of your unrealized dreams? Who will care for you if you are hurt giving birth to me?" He cannot ask her about grocery bills and doctors visits, neonatal care and post-partum depression, for she does not yet know about these things herself.

If he ever gets to see the eyes that match her troubled heart, he will love her and submit entirely to her care. She will be his mother, and he will be her little boy. She will answer some of his questions, and together they will have many more.

The LORD gives wisdom. Prov. 2:6

■ **that God would enable young people to refrain from sexuality outside of marriage, and resist peer pressure**

■ **for those whose culture demands young marriage and young motherhood, pray that God would give wisdom and understanding to the teenage parents on how to bring up their children**

Make friends with an underage mother. Discover how you can support her.

Prayer**Day** : 19

Honor Killings

Definition

Honor killings are committed by male family members against women who are perceived to have brought dishonor upon the family.[1]

■ There are around 5,000 honor killings a year.[2]

■ In Turkey, a young woman's throat was slit in the town square because a love ballad had been dedicated to her over the radio.[3]

■ Every day in Pakistan at least three women are victims of honor killings, many of whom are only guilty of being raped. This accumulated to 1,349 women in 2004.[4]

■ Honor killings are virtually ignored by community members. In many cases, the women are buried in unmarked graves and all records of their existence are wiped out.[5]

see   know   feel   pray   do

Personal Impact Story

Sudha lays in bed every night next to her husband, the man who killed their child. It has been several weeks now, but still she cannot escape the two images burned into her consciousness:

Their 17-year old daughter, Anita, lying in the bathtub, throat cut, and stab wounds all over her body. Blood running off her husband's hands in the bathroom sink.

"I had to do it," he said, his back to her, the red water flowing over white porcelain. "For her sake as well as ours." He looked at her and she saw that his eyes were dry, his mouth set in an angry line. "It was her own fault," he said, turning back to the sink and taking up a bar of soap.

Sudha, a good Muslim wife, understands, and hates herself for it. Hates herself also for the way she pushed Anita away when the girl came home, crying, her clothes torn, hair dishevelled, a cut on her forehead trickling blood into a swollen, blackened eye. Sudha can still hear the desperation in Anita's voice as she cried out to her parents.

They raped me. I tried to get away from them, but there were too many. I tried not to let them do it.

Anita's father had slapped her then, yelled at her. "Slut! You seduced them! You've shamed the whole family." Anita fell to the floor, sobbing, and Sudha wanted to reach out to her then, to take her in her arms, but she did not. She obediently followed her husband out of the room, saying nothing to her daughter, hardening her heart to the girl's pleas.

Two days later, Anita was dead.

Now Sudha's dreams are nightmares in which she sees Anita standing before her, trying to cry out, but no sound comes out of her mouth. When Sudha looks more closely, she sees why – her throat is a wide, gaping wound.

Sudha wakes up weeping, choked by her own silent screams as her husband turns over in his sleep.

GOD is the glorious one. Honor belongs to him. Is. 42:8

pray

■ **that God would show his glory to men that they might fear him and value their wives and daughters as much as themselves**

■ **that police officers would act according to laws that uphold human rights and dignity**

■ **for the establishment of women's places of refuge**

act **Research honor killings and discuss it with three different people.**

PrayerDay : 20

Prostitution

Definition

Prostitution is the sale of sexual services for money. Many trafficked girls and women start out in cheap brothels where they are broken in through a process of rapes and beatings. This process is called "seasoning."[1]

- 2 million girls between ages 5 and 15 are introduced into the commercial sex market each year.[2]

- 89% of prostitutes want to escape. 60 to 75% have been raped.

- At least 200,000 women and children work in prostitution in Thailand. 1/3 of the women are under the age of 18, and girls as young as six years old work in prostitution.[4]

- "I found myself dancing at a club at the age of 11... I have had different kinds of customers, foreigners and Filipinos. I tried suicide, but it didn't work so I turned to drugs. I want to die before my next birthday."[5]

- One time, a doctor counted 35 men using a girl in one hour. When the police raided the brothel, they found dozens of empty boxes of condoms, each box having held a thousand condoms.[6]

Personal Impact Story

It's four in the afternoon in the resort town of Pattaya, Thailand. Business is slow under the haze of the setting sun, but Yui isn't worried. She knows that once night falls there will be plenty of work. She sits behind the counter of the open-air Lucky Bar on Soi 7, chatting with other girls. They are doing each other's hair and makeup. Sometimes they will call out to the men passing by, offering drinks and good times, but the evening is too young.

Yui is not from Pattaya. She left her home in Chiang Mai when she was 16 because her parents had no money. She never went to school, so she did what uneducated, poor women in Thailand do to make money – and she did it well. She has many customers at the Lucky Bar. Sometimes though, she misses her home. She hasn't seen her family in years, and has forgotten what her mother's face looks like.

Thoughts of an increasingly distant past fade as Yui spots a group of men. They are farang – foreigners. They will have lots of money. Yui puts on her best smile and waves to them. They are all wearing rings on their left hands, except one. One of the men says something to the others, and they all laugh as they walk over to the bar. Yui speaks a little English, most of it learned from the men who pay her to have sex with them. She leans close to one of the men as she hands him his drink, and then brushes his hair back from his forehead with her fingertips. "You very handsome" she says, almost in a whisper. He looks at her and smiles.

Later that night, when she is lying beside him and listening to his snores, she will imagine, as she often does, that he falls in love with her. Then he will marry her and take her away from Pattaya, back to his country. They will have a big house and a big car. Then she will have plenty of money. She won't have to go with another stranger.

She falls asleep, still dreaming.

GOD is a righteous judge. Ps. 7:11

pray
- **that God would reveal that sexual intimacy is a reflection of his blessing and not a commodity to be bought or sold**
- **that God would destroy this exploitation and degradation of women**
- **for businesses that create alternative incomes for prostitutes**

act **Form a group of people, go and present a rose to the prostitutes you meet in your city.**

Prayer**Day** : 21

War

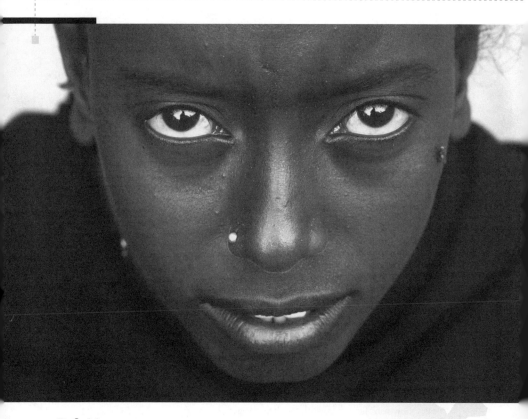

Definition

War is the waging of armed conflict against an enemy.

- The primary victims of today's wars are civilian women and their children, not soldiers.[1]

- Rape has been widely used as a weapon of war. Women have been deliberately infected with HIV/AIDS or raped pregnant. They have been used as means to undermine, disgrace and threaten the perceived enemy.[2]

- Thousands of girls in Uganda have been abducted to serve as soldiers, domestic servants and sexual slaves. In Angola, up to 30,000 girls were abducted by armed forces during its civil war.[3] Girls are often obliged to be sex slaves or "soldiers wives."[4]

- Torture of women frequently includes sexual violence with a view to humiliating and degrading the victim. Additional consequences are STD's, forced abortion, or sterilization.[5]

Personal Impact Story

We heard them coming. My husband was waiting by the door, peering outside and the light shone on him in a single ragged line, cutting him in half. He was sweating. The children were frightened and crying. I tried to muffle the sounds of their fear by pressing them close to me, but their bodies would not stop shaking. Suddenly my husband jumped away from the door, and dashed toward me, hissing, "They're here... run! Run!"

But there was nowhere to go.

They surrounded us in our own house, closing in like hungry hyenas. The leader shouted an order and they grabbed my husband. I screamed, but it was too late. They pointed the gun at my husband's head and shot him, in front of us. I tried to fight, but it was impossible. The leader motioned to his men, and two of them held me down while he raped me. I struggled, but they were all too strong for me. I saw my children being dragged outside by the other guards, screaming. I cried out, and the man on top of me cursed as he slapped my face. Then the guards beat me. They punched my face with their fists, and hit me with their rifles. "Please," I gasped. "Please. Stop. Don't hurt my children. Where are my children?" My mind was swirling with blackness and pain, my mouth was full of blood, and my eyes were swollen. My face was wet, but where the tears ended and the blood began I could not say.

I don't know how long they stayed. It could have been a few minutes or a few hours. Time means nothing when you are in hell.

They took my daughter with them. I have not seen her since. My son's body was found the next day, two kilometres away from our house, on the side of the street. He was 11 years old. My daughter was 9. I live with my sister and her husband now. I cannot sleep at night. In the daytime I cannot stop crying, because I still hear their voices, their screams and I am powerless to help them. Men despise me and women avoid me in the streets, for I have dishonoured myself and what is left of my family, allowing myself to be raped. So I stay inside the house, hidden away from their eyes, alone in a darkness that swallows my heart a little more every day.

Soon darkness will be all that's left.

GOD sent his son to be the Prince of Peace. Is 9:6

pray
- **that the kingdom of God would be established in peace and that it would protect those most vulnerable**
- **for Christian diplomats to be peacemakers**
- **for Christian counselors to help process the grief and hatred**

act **Study one hot spot of war and pray into this region.**

Africa

Definition

Africa has a population of 891 million people, with the highest birthrate of any continent. Africa is projected to grow to 2 billion people by 2050. Women in sub-Saharan Africa bear an average of 6 children. Life expectancy is low for example, the average woman only lives to be 34 in Sierra Leone and 37 in Zambia.[1]

- Almost 14 million of the 18 million women living with HIV/AIDS worldwide live in sub-Saharan Africa.[2]

- 25% of the population in sub-Saharan Africa is age 4 or younger – almost two in 10 will die before reaching their fifth birthday.[3]

- An estimated 24 million girls are deprived of an elementary school education across Africa.[5]

- Females in Zambia have little hope for a future; 50% of pregnant women are HIV positive.[6]

- Approximately 1000 girls aged between 14 and 24 are trafficked from Mozambique to work as prostitutes in South Africa each year.[7]

see   know   feel   pray   do

Personal Impact Story

The sun rules the land of the Rift Valley. As it beats down, it shapes destinies, presides over the rise and fall of chiefs, and regulates the passing of time. Again it rises over the dusty horizon, and catches in its rays a fifteen 15-year-old girl named Fana.

Fana was conceived under the village's lone tree. For hours the men had chanted and jumped. The unmarried girls had chattered and flirted. The ritual dance was over and Fana's life started just minutes later.

Her mother was unmarried. News of her pregnancy spread around the village. The birth of Fana was a proud moment. Her mother proved she could have children! She now would be able to get married.

From the time of her birth, Fana's life was hard. Her stepfather did not like her. The only education she received was learning how to scratch muddy water from the dry riverbed, or gather enough food to feed the family.

But the "days of joy" came...for the rest of the family. When her stepbrother married, Fana resolved, "I will show my love by withstanding the lash of the whip!" During the celebration the ritual whipping cut through skin into muscle and made her back bleed. She doesn't whimper or say a word except, "Hit me again"! Scars become beauty marks.

Four months ago the village had another ritual dance. This time Fana selected the man she always wanted. That night Fana conceived under the village's lone tree. Now her tummy begins to ripen. Fana is excited. Finally she will be able to marry!

Unfortunately the good-looking man gave her more than a child. He gave her HIV. Fana will die before her child reaches the age of 4. Her child will be another outcast.

As the sun descends on the western horizon, it weeps. Africa diminishes. AIDS, tribal conflict and destructive customs progressively destroy a continent. For all its strength, the sun is not able to change the life of one young women or her child.

pray

GOD loves Africa. He wants to give this continent hope and a future. Jer. 29:11

- that God would reveal the fullness of his gospel to Africa, that it has power to transform every sphere of society
- for godly men and women to live pure lives

act

Become an agent of transformation by taking a short term outreach to Africa.

PrayerDay : 23

Rape

Definition
Rape is the crime of forcing another person to submit to sex acts, especially sexual intercourse.[1]

■ Globally, 1 out of 3 women has experienced rape or sexual assault.[2]

■ Every 2 minutes, someone is sexually assaulted in America.[3]

■ "Some of them have knives and other sharp objects inserted in them after they've been raped, while others have pistols shoved into their vaginas and the triggers pulled back" said Dr. Denis Mukwege Mukengere (the lone physician at a hospital in the Congo).[4]

■ 40-60% of sexual assaults are committed against girls younger than 16.[5]

■ In South Africa a women is raped on average every 17 seconds.[6]

Personal Impact Story

I smooth her hair under my hand, and all the while I'm praying for her, silently.

Please God, let her sleep tonight. Please give her good dreams. Please keep the nightmares away. She is afraid to fall asleep, afraid of the dark. Twenty-four years old, she lies down with her head in my lap as though she were a child, and trembles as the night wears on.

I can see the marks on her arms where she's cut herself with the razor blade again, thin red lines criss-crossing her tanned skin, punishing the body for making him burn with desire. She never remembers doing it, afterward.

Please God, help her to forget for just one night…
But I know that she won't forget, not ever – the events of that dark night a year ago have made an indelible mark on her soul, just like the razor blade has on her arms.

Eventually her exhaustion causes her to drift off into an uneasy doze. Her eyes are closed, but her body is tense and keeps twitching. Sometimes she whimpers. When she does, I stroke her hair again and whisper soothing words, but though the whimpering stops for awhile, her body never relaxes.

Once, she described the nature of her recurring nightmare:
The darkness is all around, gaping like a silent howl, and he is in the center of it, coming for me. I try to run, but he is faster and grabs my shirt, pulling on it so hard that it tears. I fall to the ground, but the earth opens, and I fall into the hole, I can't stop falling. The darkness is closing around me, but I'm almost happy, because I think I've gotten away, until suddenly I feel him on top of me again. Then I understand that he IS the darkness, and I will never escape because he is everywhere. I scream as the darkness swallows me, but there is no one to hear.

When she wakes up from the nightmare, she has to run to the bathroom and vomit.

I'm praying that it will be different tonight, that she will be free of him just this once. I look down at her, gently massaging the tightened muscles in her back, willing her rigid body to ease itself into restfulness. Sleep, I think. Dawn is coming soon.

GOD hates robbery and iniquity! Is. 61:8
- ■ that God would restore robbed innocence and purity
- ■ that God would expose the selfishness of man's heart
- ■ for the multiplication of biblical support groups
- ■ that the church would raise up and address this issue

Study how purity and innocence can be restored. Discuss your discoveries with your co-workers.

Prayer**Day** : 24

Dowry

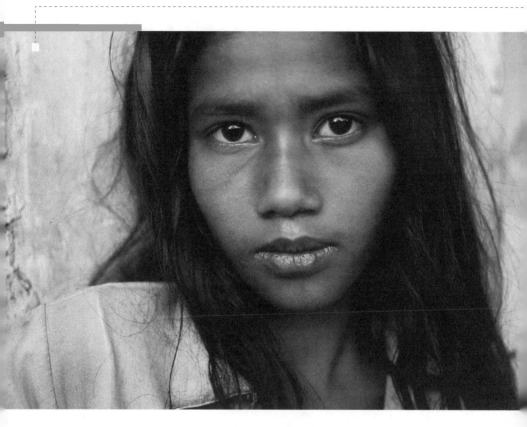

Definition

Dowry is a gift of money or valuables given by the bride's family to the family of the groom before, during or after the wedding.[1]

- Dowry was originally designed to safeguard the women. Today it is the price tag for the groom and a noose for the bride.[2]

- The average dowry is equivalent to five times the annual family income. High wedding costs and dowries are the major causes of indebtedness among India's poorest.[3]

- Since 1961 the practice of dowry has been prohibited in India. Despite this, every 21 minutes a woman is burned to death over dowry – 25,000 each year.[4]

- Many young women whose dowry is not up to the perceived standard are tortured until their parents give into the demands.[5]

- A woman is often forbidden to marry if her family is too poor to afford any dowry.[6]

Personal Impact Story

Shikha stands at the stove, frying samosas for dinner. As she watches the hot oil, she wonders if it will happen today, the splash of kerosene on her skin just before she hears the lighting of the match. She imagines her skin, blistering in the flames, and pictures her husband's face as he watches her burn to death. Shikha listens to the oil splutter in the pan, covering the clamor of the TV next door. It was a "wedding gift" from her parents to Ravi – along with a motor scooter, three new linen suits, and an entire bedroom suite. She knows these gifts are the price her parents paid for the privilege of getting their daughter "off their hands." But now Ravi wants more – more than her parents had agreed to, more than they can afford. They ask for time to meet his demands, but he is getting impatient, so he beats her. Shikha remembers their last fight, he shoved her against the doorframe, face first. When she fell, he kicked and punched her as she writhed on the floor, using his fist when he missed her with his foot.

"Worthless!" he shouted. "A good-for-nothing whore!" His voice became a hiss as he grabbed her hair and yanked it back, forcing her to look up at him. "If your family won't pay, you will."

Her body still shows the bruises from that encounter. Once she went to her parents for help, when Ravi was at work, but they would not take her back. "You belong to Ravi now," they say. "Don't make trouble. He is a good match." A match, yes. Waiting to burst into an unquenchable fire. Only she will be the one consumed in the flames. He will tell the authorities it was an accident. That's what Anja's in-laws said last year, when Anja was found, a charred corpse lying in the kitchen. "The stove must have caught fire," they said, and the investigator believed them, or at least pretended to. Shikha turns one of the samosas, and jerks her hand back suddenly as the oil spatters, burning her. She turns on the faucet and puts her wrist under the running water, biting her lip as the tears spill over at last, cool rivers on her cheeks.

GOD is love. His agape love is unconditional. 1 John 4:16b

pray
- **that the custom of dowry would be eliminated**
- **that God would reveal that love cannot be bought but that it is a gift**
- **for the reformation of India**
- **that the government of India would enforce its laws**

act **Study about dowry. Send an email to some of your friends who you think would be interested in addressing this issue.**

Prayer**Day** : 25

Missing Women

Definition

Missing means unable to be found. Women are missing mostly because of selective abortions, food deprivation, negligence, and trafficking.[1]

- Up to 200 million women worldwide are demographically "missing". Every year, up to 3 million women lose their lives as a result of gender-based violence or neglect.[2]

- About 74 million women are missing in South Asia.[3]

- "We don't kill dogs and cats as often as female children," a woman confessed to an editor for the Indian Express in Delhi.[4]

- Swiss Ambassador Theodor Winkler said the number of women who die because of gender-related violence, deprivation and discrimination is larger than the casualty toll of all the wars of the 20th century combined.[5]

Personal Impact Story

There is a void in Lakshmi's heart, where her daughter should have been. Her baby girl, Aruna – a name that meant, "dawn." But there was never any dawn for Aruna. Lakshmi never tells Raj how she feels. She knows he will not understand. "We cannot afford to raise a girl," he would say. "Boys are better – look, we have a son! Don't you care about him?" And of course Lakshmi does care. Her boy is wonderful, full of laughter and energy. He is a good boy and she is proud of him.

But Lakshmi cannot keep herself from wondering what Aruna might have been like. She pictures her beautiful, with long black hair and dark eyes. Perhaps she would have been an artist, just as Lakshmi had once secretly hoped to be. Lakshmi would have taken delight in praising her daughter's scribbles. Maybe Aruna would have won awards in school, like her brother. Of course, Lakshmi knows that they probably would not have sent Aruna to school. Education was too expensive to waste on a girl.

Lakshmi remembers sitting on her bed when she was about 20 weeks pregnant. Her stomach just beginning to show the new life. She was looking at the advertisement for a gender-detection clinic that Raj had cut out of the newspaper.

"Pay 600 rupees now, save 50,000 later", the ad said, referring to the cost of marrying off a daughter in India. Lakshmi's father-in-law once said to her, "Raising a girl is like watering someone else's garden. What's the point?"

The night before the operation, Lakshmi dreamed that she held Aruna in her arms. Her hair was so long it wrapped around her like a sari, and her eyes were closed. When she opened her eyes, Lakshmi cried out and awoke – empty sockets stared back at her.

Afterward, Lakshmi's friends comforted her, saying it was the only thing she could have done. From their childhood they were told that aborting a girl is like "cleansing the rice from maggots." They would have done it themselves in her place. Some of them had. But Lakshmi finds no comfort in their hollow words, and the empty ache inside her never goes away.

GOD created male and female to reflect his image. Gen. 1:26

pray
- **that all gender related killings would become a thing of the past**
- **that all selective abortions would stop**
- **that God would save lives today**

act
Log into a chat room on the internet and start talking about this hidden topic to people from other nations.

Education

Definition
Formal education is a conscious effort by human society to impart the skills and modes of thoughts considered essential for social functioning.[1]

- Of the world's nearly one billion illiterate adults, two-thirds are women.[2]

- Two-thirds of the 130 million children worldwide who are not in school are girls.[3]

- Girls' education may be the single most effective weapon in the prevention of HIV/AIDS. The infection rates are doubled among young people who do not finish primary school.[4]

- Education is a key economic asset for individuals and for nations. Failure to educate girls and women perpetuates needless hunger.[5]

Personal Impact Story

"But I want to go, too, Aba! I want to go to school with Negasi!"

Wagaye's father smiles indulgently at his young daughter, eleven years old. "Sweet child, you don't need to go to school. Leto is a boy. He must learn so that he can have a good job and be a good man. But you can help your mother. Don't you want to help your mother?" When Wagaye shook her head, her father laughed. "Of course you do! And one day, you will have your own family, your own beautiful children." He kisses her forehead. "You will be a good woman taking care of them."

The little girl jerks her head away and stares at the ground. Ever since Negasi began making the long walk to the main road, where he catches a bus to the schoolhouse in the next town, she has felt a deep longing in her heart to follow. But she is never allowed. Her parents want her to marry Agu, their neighbors' boy. They are already planning the wedding, which if all goes according to plan will take place on Wagaye's 13th birthday.

Wagaye runs from her father, into the cool darkness of the small house where her family lives. Her mother is inside, working hard preparing a pot of doro wat, the spicy stew they will eat for the evening meal. She looks up as her daughter's silhouette blocks the light of the sun in the doorway.

"Ah, Wagaye," she says. "Come and help me." The child goes silently to her mother's side. The woman looks at her face. "What is wrong, daughter?" "I want to go to school, but no one lets me."

The woman says nothing. She puts down the spoon and turns her gaze toward the window. Outside, her husband is standing in the road, laughing with friends who have stopped by. The woman sighs.

"Don't cry, Wagaye," she says at last, softly. She begins stirring once more. "No one let me go either."

GOD shows no partiality! Deut. 10:7

pray
- that God would open the minds of leaders and fathers to enable their women and daughters to receive education
- for the release of more teachers, school buildings and biblical curriculum

act
Do you know any schoolteachers? Encourage them to invest their holidays in developing countries to teach girls. Join them!

PrayerDay : 27

Single Mothers

Definition

Single mothers are female parents or custodians who provide primary care for one or more children alone. They often work more than 40 hours a week while carrying the full responsibility of cooking, cleaning, and nurturing the future generation.

- 57% of single mothers are living below the poverty line. For those who are younger than 25, this number increases to 85%.[1]
- 78% of all single mothers are employed. 45% of them hold down more than one job.[2]
- There are 10 million single mothers living with children under 18 in the USA.[3]

Personal Impact Story

Pam has already hit the snooze button twice. She hits it four more times before she rolls out of bed. Those twenty full extra minutes of uninterrupted time allows her to loiter in and out of sleep. She could use a strong cup of coffee but is afraid she might get another migraine. She can't afford to miss another day of work this month. Pam goes through her mental list, another early morning ritual. She thinks through all the activities of the day, once the kids are fed, cleaned, dressed, and in the car:

- drop Chelsea off at Day Care, make her promise only to phone me at work if it's an emergency
- drop Tanner off at school
- stand behind a cash register for eight hours
- pick up the kids, promise them they won't have to go to after-school Day Care much longer
- take the kids to swimming lessons, resist fear of drowning
- dinner (make something quick)
- drive-thru at McDonald's if/when Tanner refuses to eat
- fight the urge to swear or cry in front of the kids
- help Tanner with his homework – how can they give homework to a seven year old?
- convince Tanner homework is more important than cartoons
- give Chelsea a bath and tuck her into bed, pray to God she doesn't ask again "when is dad coming home?"'

The alarm clock rings for the sixth time. Pam forgets her abbreviated list for the moment. She can hear the TV from the other room. Tanner is already awake. Pam tramps to the bathroom and looks at herself in the mirror. She wishes she could wash the last three years out of her face. She pulls her hair back into a ponytail, and pouts. Her body is slipping away. She makes eye contact with herself, only briefly, then watches her own lips move as she wonders out loud, "What happened to you, girl?"

Pam sucks in her cheeks and tosses her hair, pretends to be young again, then laughs. "Better make that cup of coffee," she mutters. "It's only Monday."

GOD is a father to the fatherless. Ps. 68:5

- **that God would strengthen single mothers**
- **that God would correct neglectful fathers**
- **for male teachers and family members to fill in the gap left by the missing fathers**
- **for the multiplication of organizations that promote family values**

Get to know a single mother at your church. Help out where possible.

PrayerDay : 28

Iran

Definition

Iran is a nation of 34 million women who face discrimination simply because they are female.[1]

- Iran has one of the highest records of runaway girls and women worldwide, an estimated 300,000. Most of them are raped within the first 24 hours of their departure.[2]

- Sleeping with a 9-year-old girl is legitimized by religion as a legal marriage. Battering women is dignified by reference to verses in the Koran.[3]

- In 9 months of 2005, 150 Kurdish women committed suicide, the majority by setting themselves on fire. Domestic violence, social injustice, and discrimination are cited as the main reasons.[4]

- In 2005, a 16-year old girl was hung publicly and a 13-year old girl was sentenced to be stoned to death. Six more are on death row.[5]

- There has been a 635% increase in the number of teenage girls in prostitution. About 84,000 women and girls live on the streets or in the 250 brothels of Tehran.[6]

know   feel   pray   do

Personal Impact Story

Exhausted, Ghazal set down her pack and crouched behind a rock to rest. This time she must stay hidden from view. The camp she tries to reach must surely be on the other side of this valley.

The sun still shimmers in the late afternoon. Below her is an open grassy slope. She was close enough now that if she walked down to the bottom of the valley Ghazal would surely be spotted on the bare hillside. She would risk crossing the road at night and find a place to hide on the other side tomorrow. She must stay hidden at all costs.

Grimly she remembered the first time she'd run away. She had thought her home was bad but the men who found her that night were far worse. They used her as a toy, stripping her of any dignity. When they were finished they threw a filthy blanket over her to cover her nakedness, but nothing could cover the shame she would carry for the rest of her life. Unprotected, helpless, and hurt she fell into the hands of a man that treated her as a slave. Ghazal was forced to work and answer his every call. She took her first chance to escape knowing she had no place to go, but the rumor of a camp kept her tortured body moving. She was determined to find them.

She had heard about this camp from a girl that had whispered it to her one night. That girl was dead now. Stoned for adultery, though Ghazal knew that she couldn't possibly have been guilty. That very night they had huddled together in the shack where he had kept them. The girl had talked about the camp as though she herself were thinking of making a run. The dream of not being mistreated, but taught how to fight was all that she could cling to.

This time she would make it. She would join these warriors in place of that other girl. She would fight. That's what she wanted. She would fight and die a martyr. She leaned back against her pack and closed her eyes.

If she could just find these freedom fighters…

pray

There is no longer a distinct value for male over female for we are all one in Christ Jesus. Gal. 3:28

- ■ **that God would correct the value system of Iran**
- ■ **that God would comfort Iranian women who suffer injustice**
- ■ **for the multiplication of women's shelters all over Iran**

act

Start praying regularly with a prayer partner for the spread of the gospel in Iran.

PrayerDay : 29

Slavery

Definition
Slavery is forced labor. For women and children this includes being sold for prostitution or debt bondage, used in pornography or armed conflict or being harvested for human organs.[1]

- There are over 27 million slaves in the world today.[2]
- There are 218 million working children between the ages of 5 and 17.[3]
- An estimated 100,000 women and children are forced to enter the sex trade in the United States each year.[4]
- Children aged 7 to 10 work 12 to 14 hours a day, are paid less than one-third of the adult wage and are vulnerable to sexual and physical abuse.[5]

Personal Impact Story

Honey is in her seat on the airplane. It is the first time she's flown anywhere. Biting her lip, nervous and excited, imagining what her new life will be like. If she knew what awaited her, she would take one deep, final breath and ask God to hurl the airplane into the sea.

Australia. She saw pictures of the country when she was young. Honey and her little sister liked the photographs of baby koala bears and dreamed of touching their soft fur. Hopped around the street like kangaroos, giggling until their sides hurt. Met Australian travelers on the streets of Bangkok, tourists visiting Thailand to take photos of temples and rickshaws that they would later show to little Australian children.

The person sitting beside her is more devil than man. Once the plane touches Australian soil he will casually lean into Honey's seat and say words he has whispered to other young, hopeful girls. Plans have changed. She will not be working as a maid in a home with children. There is no factory job waiting for her in Sydney. The seat belt sign will turn off and Honey will realize she's been fooled. The exciting job opportunity, the promise of a brighter future in another country, was too good to be true.

Australia. Land of childhood fantasy where Honey will become a new worker in a thriving sex-trade. Where she will be forced to sell her body day after day for years to pay for her newly acquired debt: airplane ticket, visa, passport, luggage, clothing, travel documents. The very things promised to her as part of a lucrative job contract.

Honey sips on orange juice and looks out the window at the sky. Makes shapes out of the clouds. Turns and looks at the employment agent in the seat beside her who helped her out of the bleak situation at home in Thailand. Not realizing that within hours he will confiscate her passport and lock her into her new home – a small apartment shared with four other girls. That, within a few hours he will introduce her to her owner, the first man who will rape her in her new country. Within a few hours she will be faced with her new fate: forced sex with johns every day, hospital visits, bruises to the bone, involuntary abortions, and a debt that won't go away. The memory of home, anger at her naïveté. Anger that she let hope get the better of her. The desire to escape.

Honey in her seat on the airplane. Excitedly biting her lip. Imagining her new life.

GOD is the redeemer of those in slavery! Deut. 7:8
- ■ that God would end slavery in our lifetime
- ■ for the redemption of those trapped in slavery
- ■ that the media would expose slavery

Research one slavery hotspot. Challenge the ambassador of that nation to enforce their anti-slavery laws.

Prayer**Day** : 30

End Notes

CHILD PROSTITUTION
Personal Impact Story written by Andrew Kooman

1. www.polity.org.za/html/govdocs/white_papers/social97gloss.html
2. http://globalfundforchildren.org/pdfs/GFC_childtraffic_prost.pdf
3. Pusurinkham, Sirirat. "A Globe of Witnesses." http://www.thewitness.org/agw/pusurinkham.121901.html) Child Prostitution in Thailand
4. Bolowana, Angela. 2004. The Mercury "40,000 Child Prostitutes 'Street Children Vulnerable to Sex Trade'" Edition 1
5. http://www.ecpatusa.org/travel_tourism.asp

AIDS
Personal Impact Story written by Grace Farag

1. www.wordnet.princeton.edu/perl/webwn
2. "HIV/AIDS." Colors Magazine Volume 67. 2006: p3,64, 87, 88-90.
3. Ibid.
4. Ibid.
5. Ibid.
6. Ibid.

5. http://hrw.org/campaigns/pakistan/forms.htm
6. Ibid.

ABORTION
Personal Impact Story written by Andrew Kooman

1. www.wordreference.com/definition/abortion
2. "Facts in Brief: Induced Abortion Worldwide, 2003," Alan Guttmacher Institute. http://www.abortionaccess.org/AAP/publica_resources/fact_sheets/illegalabortion.htm
3. "Abortion: Tune into the Truth." 2004. http://www.abortiontv.com/Misc/AbortionStatistics.htm
4. "Unsafe Abortion Around the World." 2006. http://www.plannedparenthood.org/pp2/portal/files/portal/medicalinfo/abortion/fact-abortion-unsafe.xml
5. "An Overview of Abortion in the US." 2006. http://www.guttmacher.org/presentations/abort_slides.pdf

REFUGEES
Personal Impact Story written by Andrew Kooman

1. http://web.amnesty.org/pages/refugees-background-eng#refugee
2. http://www.unicef.org.nz/school-room/refugees/facts-on refugees.html

DOMESTIC VIOLENCE
Personal Impact Story written by Andrew Kooman

1. http://www.helpguide.org/mental/domestic_violence_abuse_types_signs_causes_effects.htm#definition
2. Hayzer, Noeleen. "Violence Against Women Around The World." Executive director, UNIFEM http://www.zonta.org/site/DocServer/Violence_Against_Women_Around_the_World_Zontian_April_20.pdf?docID=604
3. http://www.letswrap.com/dvinfo/stats.htm
4. Ibid.
5. www.hrw.org/reports/1999/pakistan/Pakhtml-05.htm
6. Hayzer, Noeleen. "Violence Against Women Around The World." Executive director, UNIFEM http://www.zonta.org/site/DocServer/Violence_Against_Women_Around_the_World_Zontian_April_20.pdf?docID=604

PAKISTAN
Personal Impact Story written by Steven Schoenoff

1. http://www.yespakistan.com/people/missing_women.asp
2. ANAA Voice. www.anaavoice.org/article-print-18.html
3. http://web.amnesty.org/library/Index/engASA330181999
4. Farooq, Mohammad Omar. "Rape and Hudood Ordinance: Perversions of Justice in the Name of Islam". http://www.globalwebpost.com/farooqm/writings/gender/rape_fiqh.html

3. www.un.org/ecosocdev/geninfo/women/women96.htm
4. www.un.org/rights/dpi1772e.htm
5. http://web.amnesty.org/pages/refugees-background-eng#refugee

EATING DISORDERS
Personal Impact Story written by Andrew Kooman

1. www.answers.com/topic/eating-disorder
2. The Renfrew Center Foundation for Eating Disorders, "Eating Disorders 101 Guide: A Summary of Issues, Statistics and Resources," published September 2002, revised October 2003, http://www.renfrew.org
3. http://www.state.sc.us/dmh/anorexia/statistics.htm
4. Renfrew Center.2006. www.eatingdisorderscoalition.org/reports/statistics.html
5. "Food Safety and Food Borne Illness." http://www.inch-aweigh.com/dietstats.htm

PURDAH
Personal Impact Story written by Andrew Kooman

1. http://en.wikipedia.org/wiki/Purdah
2. "Purdah." http://departments.kings.edu/womens_history/purdah.html
3. Ibid.
4. Ibid.
5. Ibid. and 6. Ibid.

FEMALE LABORERS

Personal Impact Story written by Andrew Kooman

1. http://www.unfpa.org/swp/2005/presskit/factsheets/facts_gender.htm
2. http://www.un.org/ecosocdev/geninfo/women/women96.htm
3. www.caa.org.au/publications/iid/TWW
4. Department of Economic and Social Affairs. Statistics Division. Progress towards the Millennium Development Goals, 1990-2005. Available at: http://unstats.un.org/unsd/mi/goals_2005/goal_3.pdf
5. www.thp.org/reports/indiawom.htm

CHINA

Personal Impact Story written by Andrew Kooman

1. http://english.people.com.cn/200112/28/eng20011228_87658.shtml
2. Glenn, David. "A Dangerous Surplus of Sons?" 2004. http://chronicle.com/free/v50/i34/34a01401.htm
3. http://www.msnbc.msn.com/id/5953508
4. Bailey, Ronald. "Sexing Babies." 2004. http://www.reason.com/rb/rb100604.shtml

BARREN WOMEN

Personal Impact Story written by Grace Farag

1. www.dict.die.net/barren
2. "Infertility A Worldwide Problem." http://www.ein.org/general.htm
3. Geary, Deborah "Global Infertility" http://preconception.com/resources/articles/globalinfertility.htm
4. Sembuya, Rita. 2003. http://www.ashoka.org/fellows/viewprofile3.cfm?reid=144024
5. http://www.childinfo.org/eddb/fertility/index.htm
6. http://www.ein.org/general.htm

PORNOGRAPHY

Personal Impact Story written by Andrew Kooman

1. http://www.media-awareness.ca/english/resources/educational/overheads/ethics/definition_pornography.cfm
2. http://internet-filter-review.toptenreviews.com/internet-pornography-statistics.html
3. Ibid.
4. Ibid.
5. www.tecrime.com/llartp71.htm
6. http://internet-filter-review.toptenreviews.com/internet-pornography-statistics.html

5. Baculinao, Eric. "China Grapples With Legacy of Its 'Missing Girls.'" 2004. http://www.msnbc.msn.com/id/5953508
6. All-China Women's Federation (ACWF) http://english.people.com.cn/200303/09/eng20030309_112987.shtml

INCEST

Personal Impact Story written by Andrew Kooman

1. www.mercksource.com/pp/us/cns/cns_hl_dorlands.jspzQzpgzEzzSzppdocszSzuszSzcommonzSzdorlandszSzdorlandzSzdmd_i_05zPzhtm
2. http://www.womenofsubstance.org/sexabuse.htm
3. http://www.yellodyno.com/html/rape_stats.html
4. http://www.womenofsubstance.org/sexabuse.htm
5. "Study: East African Girls Born to High Risk" 2006. http://www.pambazuka.org/en/category/wgender/34564
6. http://www.childhelpusa.org/resources/learning-center/statistics
7. www.icasa.org/uploads/ adult_survivors_of_child_sexual_abuse_-_DRAFT-7.doc
8. http://www.childhelpusa.org/resources/learning-center/statistics

FEMALE SUICIDE BOMBERS

Personal Impact Story Written by Grace Farag

1. Victor, Barbara. "Army of Roses: Inside the World of Palestinian Women Suicide Bombers." (London: Constable and Robinson, 2004.)
2. Ibid.
3. Ibid.
4. Ibid.
5. Ibid.
6. Ibid.

STARVATION

Personal Impact Story written by Andrew Kooman

1. http://www.wordreference.com/definition/starvation
2. Shah, Anup. "Causes of Hunger are Related to Poverty." http://www.globalissues.org/TradeRelated/Poverty/Hunger/Causes.asp
3. http://www.care.org/campaigns/world-hunger/facts.asp
4. Ibid.
5. www.thp.org/reports/indiawom.htm
6. http://www.care.org/campaigns/world-hunger/facts.asp

TRAFFICKING
Personal Impact Story written by Paul Childers
1. http://www.savethechildren.net/nepal/key_issues/traffdefi-nition.html
2. http://www.unfpa.org/swp/2005/english/ch7/index.htm
3. Watts, C and C. Zimmerman. 2002. "Violence Against Women: Global Scope and Magnitude." The Lancet , Vol 359. April 6, 2002.
4. http://www.unfpa.org/swp/2005/english/ch7/index.htm
5. http://www.paralumun.com/issueseurope.htm www.ilo.org/public/english/employment/gems/download/mbook6.pdf 18.12
6. IOM Kosovo, Counter Trafficking Unit. 2001. Return and reintegration project, situation report. Pristina: IOM. International Organization for Migration (IOM). 2001. New IOM figures on the global scale of trafficking: Trafficking in Migrants Quarterly Bulletin. Geneva: IOM

AFGHANISTAN
Personal Impact Story written by Steve Schoenhoff
1. Lobe, Jim. "Iraq, Afghanistan Among Top Ten Failed Sta-tes." 2006. http://www.antiwar.com/lobe/?articleid=8935

3. www.savethechildren.org/mothers/report_2004/images/pdf/Perils_pp9_15.pdf
4. www.unicef.org/girlseducation/index_bigpicture.htm 2005

HONOR KILLINGS
Personal Impact Story written by Grace Farag
1. http://www.answers.com/topic/honor-killing
2. http://www.csmonitor.com/2005/0302/p15s01-wome.html
3. Maye, Hillary. "Thousands of Women Killed for Family Honor." 2002.http://news.nationalgeographic.com/news/2002/02/0212_020212_honorkilling.html
4. Ibid.
5. Emery, James. "Reputations is Everything: Honor Killing among the Palestinians." 2003. http://www.worldandi.com/newhome/public/2003/may/clpub.asp

PROSTITUTION
Personal Impact Story written by Grace Farag
1. www.humanrightswatch/asia1995page34
2. Human rights and Health Provider.2001.www.unfpa.org/swp/2000/english/ch03.html
3. Trafficking in Persons Report.2005.

2. "The World Fact book." 2006. www.cia.gov/cia/publica-tions/factbook/geos/af.html
3. www.unstats.un.org
4. http://www.who.int/countries/afg/en
5. http://www.hawaii.edu/global/projects_activities/Trafficking/Afghan_Women_Status.pdf
6. www.unstats.un.org
7. www.unicef.org

FEMALE GENITAL MUTILATION
Personal Impact Story written by Paul Childers
1. http://www.amnesty.org/ailib/intcam/femgen/fgm1.htm
2. www.stopfgm.org
3. Ibid.
4. http://www.who.int/reproductive-health/fgm
5. http://www.voices-unabridged.org/article2.php?id_ss_article=191&id_rub=1&sous_rub=Violence&numero=1
6. Ibid.

TEENAGE MOTHERS
Personal Impact Story written by Andrew Kooman
1. http://www.coolnurse.com/pregnancy2.htm
2. Not Just Another Single Issue: Teen Pregnancy Prevention's Link to Other Critical Social Issues, "The National Campaign to Prevent Teen Pregnancy", February 2002.

http://www.state.gov/g/tip/rls/tiprpt/2005/46606.htm
4. "Prostitution and Sex Tourism." http://www.arches.uga.edu/~haneydaw/twwh/traf.html#description, 27.12.2003
5. http://www.equalitynow.org/action_eng_12_1.html)4
6. Hughes, Donna. "The World's Sex Slaves Need Liberation, Not Condoms." 2/24/03, vol008, issue 23 http://www.uri.edu/artsci/wms/hughes/condoms_sex_slaves

WAR
Personal Impact Story written by Grace Farag
1. http://www.un.org/ecosocdev/geninfo/women/women96.htm
2. http://www.womenwarpeace.org/issues/violence/violence.htm (2000)
3. www.frontpageafrica.com
4. http://www.womenwarpeace.org/issues/violence/violence.htm (2000)

AFRICA
Personal Impact Story written by Paul Childers
1. www.cia.gov/cia/publications/factbook/geos/ct.html
2. "Gender, Race and AIDS in Africa" http://apic.igc.org/re-sources/page.php?op=read&documention=302&type=7&issues=1&campaigns=2
3. "The Plight of Women in the Sub-Saharan Africa." 2006. http://www.theolympian.com/apps/pbcs.dll/

article?AID=/20060123/LIVING0301/60123033/1076
4. "For Girls in Africa, Education is Uphill Fight." 2005.
http://www.iht.com/articles/2005/12/22/news/ethiopia.php
5. "The Plight of Women in the Sub-Saharan Africa."
www.theolympian.com/apps/pbcs.dll/
article?AID=/20060123/LIVING0301/60123033/1076
6. "Study: East African Girls Born to High Risk" 2006.
http://www.pambazuka.org/en/category/wgender/34564

RAPE
Personal Impact Story Written by Grace Farag
1. www.thefreedictionary.com/rape
2. http://www.gmu.edu/facstaff/sexual/brochures/WorldStats2005.pdf
3. www.rainn.org/statistics/indes.html
4. Koinange, Jeff. "World Rape, Brutality Ignored to Aid
Congo Peace" by Friday, May 26th 2006. www.cnn.com
5. http://www.ivillage.co.uk/newspol/camp/refuge/
articles/0,10233,186771_186926.htm
6. http://www.paralumun.com/womensissues.htm

EDUCATION
Personal Impact Story written by Grace Farag
1. www.wordreference.com/definition/education
2. http://www.un.org/ecosocdev/geninfo/women/women96.htm
3. Ibid.
4. http://www.unicef.org/media/media_4408.html
5. "Millions of Girls Still Out of School on International
Women's Day" 2006. http://www.millenniumcampaign.
org/site/apps/nl/content2.asp?c=grKVL2NLE&b=2192
63&content_id=%7B3334AFCC-CBAD-423D-85EE-
66FA0811ED6C%7D&notoc=1

SINGLE MOTHERS
Personal Impact Story written by Andrew Kooman
1. www.unece.org/stats/trend/ch2.htm
2. "Bureau of Labor Statistics." 2002-2003.
http://www.coabode.com/factsheet.php
3. http://www.census.gov/Press-Release/www/releases/archives/
facts_for_features_special_editions/006560.html

DOWRY
Personal Impact Story written by Grace Farag
1. www.en.wikipedia.org/wiki/dowry
2. "An Anthology of Writing by Students and Teachers from
South Asia." 2002.www.iearn.org/civics/pdf/book.pdf
3. www.thp.org/reports/indiawom.htm
4. Brunner, Borgna. "International Women's Day." 2006
http://www.infoplease.com/spot/womensday1.html
5. Huggler, Justin. "The Price Of Being A Woman: Slavery In
Modern India." 2006. http://www.countercurrents.org/gen-
huggler040406.htm
6. www.answers.com/topic/dowry

MISSING WOMEN
Personal Impact Story written by Grace Farag
1. "Missing Women." http://www.yespakistan.com/
people/missing_women.asp
2. Ibid.
3. Ibid.
4. Ibid.
5. Lederer, Edith. Study: Violence and discrimination against
women is a major cause of death, ranking with disease,
hunger and war, study says. 2005. http://www.hst.org.
za/news/20041036

IRAN
Personal Impact Story by Steven Schoenoff
1. "Iranian Women Seek Equality" 2000.
http://news.bbc.co.uk/1/hi/world/middle_east/643526.stm
2. http://www.iranfocus.com/modules/news/article.
php?storyid=1617
3. www.irandwr.org/english/0411/brief.htm
4. http://www.rferl.org/featuresarticle/2006/02/c43c681f-0ad1-
49b6-aadb-3784ca430536.html
5. http://www.iranfocus.com/modules/news/article.
php?storyid=1617
6. http://www.womenfreedomforum.com/indexphp?option=com_
content&task=view&id=86&Itemid=41&PHPSESSID=c1b8b5b
4ad0d4934dbd40a935eb0286f

SLAVERY
Personal Impact Story written by Andrew Kooman
1. www.unhchr.ch/html/menu6/2/fs14.htm
2. Bales,Kevin. "How Can We End Slavery?" 2003.http://magma.
nationalgeographic.com/ngm/0309/feature1/online_extra.html
3."Child Labor" http://www.antislavery.org/homepage/antislave-
ry/childlabour.htm
4. Ibid.
5. Ibid

Thanks

Many people have sacrificed to bring this booklet from concept to reality. Joey Paynter enabled us to complete this project. Thank you, for your tireless work ethic and your positive attitude. Andrew Kooman and Grace Farag wrote most of the "Personal Impact Stories." Thanks for putting your heart into it! Saara Kurtilla literally flew around the world to put this project into motion. Melissa Miller helped us with necessary research at the last minute, thank you. We would also like to thank Ralf Krauss (for the fourth time enabling our dreams to become reality), Fiona Gifford (the Connexity Conference was the start of this project), Loren and Darlene Cunningham (your example enables us to step out in faith), David and Christine Hamilton (your input was priceless), Steve Schoenhoff, Lisa Orvis, the December DTS in Oxford 2003, the Montana DTS of January 2004. Finally, we would like to thank our parents John and Yvonne Childers as well as Gerhard and Anneliese Fortenbacher for your constant support over the years.

Bookings

Over the next year and a half, we will travel all over the world spreading this message. If you are interested in having us speak in your conference, church, UofN course or any other venue, please contact us at photogenx.kona@gmail.com

Donations

If you would like to contribute financially to this project, please do one of the following:

For a tax-deductible receipt, write a check to "University of the Nations."
Please do not write a designation on the check, but include a note specifying how you want it spent. Then post it to Paul Childers, 75-5851 Kuakini Hwy #248, Kailua-Kona, HI 96740 USA.

Or you can donate online at http://www.mission-unlimited.net. Your tax-deductible receipt will be sent electronically.

If you want to support us personally, please contact us on photogenx.kona@gmail.com.

© photogenX, 2006

ISBN 1-4276-0425-8

photography | Susi Childers   design | krausswerbeagentur.de   print | druckerei-mack.de